Power Cutting

Efficient and Accurate Rotary Cutting
with Omnigrid® Tools

by Debbie Caffrey

Debbie's Creative Moments, Inc.
P. O. Box 29418
Santa Fe, NM 87592-9418

www.debbiescreativemoments.com

Acknowledgements

Thank you to Omnigrid® and the Prym-Dritz Corporation for their support and the manufacturing of such accurate, fine quality tools.

Thank you, too, to Phyllis Kent of Los Lunas, New Mexico, who once again did beautiful quilting for me on very short notice.

Power Cutting

Efficient and Accurate Rotary Cutting with Omnigrid Tools

Credits

Illustrated by

Debbie Caffrey
Santa Fe, New Mexico

Photographed by

Dan Caffrey
President of Everything
Debbie Doesn't Want to Do
Santa Fe, New Mexico

Proofread by

Erin Caffrey
Nashville, Tennessee

Printed by

Palmer Printing
St. Cloud, Minnesota

Published by

Debbie's Creative Moments, Inc.
P. O. Box 29418
Santa Fe, NM 87592-9418
USA
www.debbiescreativemoments.com

ISBN: 0-9645777-7-1

First Printing, 2003

Table of Contents

Introduction

Who should read this book?

Everyone who quilts should read this book! Rotary cutting has become an integral part of practically every form of quilting. Quilting, whether at a beginning skill level or more experienced level, uses a good deal of rotary cutting. Many books have already been written on the subject. Therefore, you may be asking why I am writing another and what is different in my approach.

Most quilters who already know how to rotary cut have not even thought about how they can improve their skills. They are still cutting the same way they did twenty-plus years ago when rotary cutting was first introduced to quilters.

Quilters who have seen me demonstrate cutting in my workshops or on television (two episodes of *Simply Quilts* on HGTV) frequently ask for a book that outlines my rotary cutting techniques. I have taught seminars to quilt shop owners and instructors who say that my cutting method is a great foundation for a series of classes.

Books containing rotary cutting are usually too general in subject matter to cover more than just the basics of rotary cutting. They cover other topics like fabric selection, piecing, quilting, and binding in greater detail than what is in this book. Although this book contains instructions for four quilts, its main focus is cutting.

What is power cutting?

Perhaps the easiest way to answer the question, "What is power cutting?", is to first tell you what it is not. Power cutting is not cutting fabric into strips by measuring one strip at a time, making a cut, moving the ruler off one strip, moving the strip, and finally, repositioning the ruler onto the fabric to measure, repeating the process for every strip you need to cut. The method I have just described results in a lot of wasted time and motion, as well as, inaccurate cutting. In addition, to avoid wavy strips when cutting as described above, the fabric must be straightened and squared after every few strips. That wastes more time *and* fabric.

Chapter Two describes power cutting step by step in great detail through the use of full color photos. In an effort to keep the size of this book manageable and to cover the subject thoroughly, the book focuses only on rotary cutting strips, squares, rectangles, and crosscutting strip pieced panels into smaller sections. There are no triangles, trapezoids, and other shapes. They will be covered in a future volume.

When reading this book, I want you to imagine that you are watching over my shoulder while I work in my studio. Take note of which rulers I use and how I move them. Notice that I choose different ways to crosscut strip pieced panels depending on the project. Now, follow me into my studio, and let's do some power cutting.

Chapter One

Basic Tools

Cutting Mat

It is necessary to have a self-healing cutting mat to protect your cutting table and prolong the life of your rotary cutter's blade. There are many brands and sizes available. I prefer the Omnigrid® 18″ x 24″ mat. It is slightly larger than 18″ x 24″ and has a true cutting area of 18″ x 24″. Most other brands that advertise the same size are really smaller by an inch in each direction. This slightly smaller size is inconvenient for cutting fat quarters.

Smaller mats, 12″ x 18″ and under, are available, and they are fine for detail cutting or taking along to classes, but they are too small for effective power cutting. The larger 24″ x 36″ mat is wonderful, but it is more expensive. If you can afford the larger mat and have space for it in your studio you may prefer to purchase it.

Most mats on the market are printed with a grid on one side. These grids are good for a quick reference or to make sure that a fabric strip is straight, but I do not use them as a guide for cutting. Instead, I use the rulers to measure, as you will see in Chapter Two. Using the ruler is more accurate and increases the lifespan of your cutting mat. No matter how good the quality of your mat, if you continually cut on the same line you will form a rut in the mat.

Most mats are made to be used on both sides. Using both sides of your cutting mat extends its lifespan. The gridded side of the Omnigrid® mat is green. The back, non-gridded side of the Omnigrid® mat is light gray. The two colors allow you to use the side that most contrasts with your fabric so that you can more easily see the edge of the fabric against the mat. Therefore, if you are cutting green fabric, use the gray side for better visibility.

Rotary Cutter

Just like cutting mats, rotary cutters come in a variety of sizes, too. The most common sizes are 18mm, 45mm, and 60mm. I suggest using the 45mm for most of your cutting. The small 18mm cutter is helpful for cutting curves. The large 60mm is useful for those of you who cut through more than eight layers of fabric. Eight layers of fabric is my "comfort zone", so the 45mm works perfectly for me.

Rotary cutters on the market today come with handles that are larger and more cushioned than the handles of the past. These rotary cutters have been designed to reduce the amount of strain and fatigue caused by cutting. If you have an old rotary cutter consider upgrading.

For safety's sake be sure to close the blade guard after every cut and before laying down the cutter. Get into the habit of closing the guard even if you are the only one in the room. Rotary cutters have a way of getting under the fabric on your cutting table. Searching for a cutter with an open blade can cause a serious injury. Omnigrid®'s cutters have a self-closing blade. In addition to the blade guard, many rotary cutters have a lock to keep the blade from opening accidentally. Be sure to use the lock when storing the cutter in a drawer or tool bag.

Do not hesitate to replace dull blades. Just as with knives, you are more likely to cut yourself with a dull blade than with a sharp one. When replacing blades, keep track of the order in which the pieces are assembled and get them back together the same way. Proper assembly makes a difference in the performance and safety of your rotary cutter.

Some rotary cutters are suitable for right-handed and left-handed cutting with no alteration. Other rotary cutters must be disassembled and have the blade moved to the other side of the cutter. These cutters come assembled for the right-handed user. Follow the directions to move the blade to the other side if you are left-handed.

Rulers

Go to any quilt shop and you will find dozens of rulers and tools designed for rotary cutting. You will need only a couple of very functional sizes to start. As you do more quilting you will discover other sizes and shapes that work best for your projects. Add additional rulers and tools as you find uses for them.

I prefer the Omnigrid® rulers. Their accuracy is unsurpassed. The logo is small and in an area where it will not interfere with the function of the ruler. The lines are fine, allowing for precise measurements, but they are still easy to read. The Omnigrid® rulers are designed to be user-friendly for both right-handed and left-handed quilters. There are black and yellow lines in both directions on the rulers. This allows you to read them on all colors and values of fabrics without repositioning them.

Chapter Two will show you how to use tools of various sizes. My 15″ square is the ruler that I use most often. The ruler that I use second most is the 6″ x 24″ ruler. These two rulers are almost indispensable for rotary cut quilts.

Beyond the two sizes mentioned above, my next recommendation would be a 6″ or 6½″ square.

Here are a few other useful rulers: A 9½″ square is handy for cutting blocks as in the Rail Fence pattern as shown on page 14. The 1″ x 6″ ruler is good for marking short stitching lines as in the Bow Tie pattern. Omnigrid® makes several rulers that have fine ⅛″ grids marked on them. I use the 4″ gridded square for small, detailed work, and I use the 3″ x 18″ gridded ruler for drafting.

Some quilters have difficulty keeping their ruler from slipping. To address this problem, Omnigrid® has a product called Invisigrip. It is a clear plastic that adheres to the back of the ruler with static cling. Using Invisigrip is easy and may increase the accuracy of your cutting. Cut a piece that is ¼″ smaller than the ruler in both directions. In other words, use a piece that measures 5¾″ x 23¾″ for your 6″ x 24″ ruler. Remove the Invisigrip from the paper and rub it onto the back of the ruler. The ruler can still be slid into place with the Invisigrip on the back of it, but with the slightest amount of pressure applied to the ruler as you hold it, the ruler does not slip.

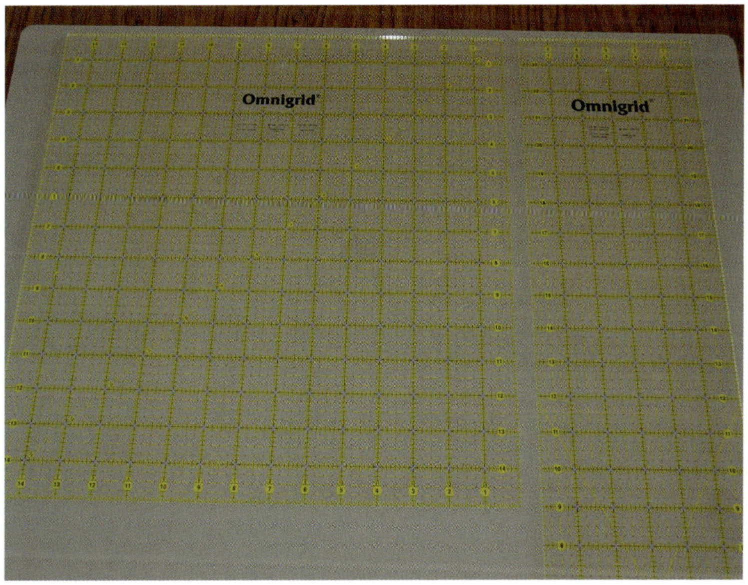

Chapter Two

Power Cutting

Setting Up the Cutting Area

There is some set-up necessary before you are ready to cut efficiently.

Your cutting surface should be approximately 4″ below your bent elbow. Sometimes when I am teaching a workshop at a hotel conference room, I go to the kitchen and ask for full #10 cans of anything they have. I put one under each leg of the banquet table to raise it to a convenient cutting height. It is a great temporary fix.

Ideally, you want to cut on a surface that is set up as an island or a peninsula so that you can get to both sides of the cutting mat. The width of the table should be 24″ to 27″. The maximum width should be 30″, which is the width of a basic banquet table. This allows you to cut from both sides of the table without constantly moving your fabric. If you must cut on a wider table (or a counter or table that is against a wall) you can rotate the mat during your cutting.

Below you will see the island that I use for cutting. I purchased it through mail order from *Ikea*. You may be lucky enough to have one of their stores near you. The island has drawers, shelves, and baskets for storing my tools and current projects. I keep the rulers that I use most frequently right on top in a ruler rack. The tools are always at my fingertips. Instead of one large cutting mat, I line up three 18″ x 24″ mats. They fit my space better and allow me the flexibility of the smaller mats.

Finally, make sure there is plenty of space. Too often quilters try to cut on a surface that is piled high with fabrics and supplies, leaving just a small corner where they can cut. Clear the area!

Folding the Fabric for Cutting

NOTE: The non-gridded side of the mat is used in most of the following photos so you will see that I am cutting according to the ruler and not the mat's grid.

In most rotary cut patterns, strips are cut across the width of the fabric, selvage to selvage, making them approximately 42″ long with selvages on each of the short ends. Prepare your fabric for cutting by folding it in half, selvage to selvage. See photo 1.

If you are having trouble folding the fabric evenly, and you are using a print fabric, look for a motif in the print that falls on the fold. Follow the repetition of this motif while you are folding the fabric along its lengthwise grain. Prints run true on the lengthwise grain, but tend to go uphill or downhill on the crosswise grain. If you are using a solid, you will have to shift the top layer of fabric to the right or left until it lays flat and the selvages are even.

Notice that the cut end of the fabric in photo 1 is very uneven. This uneven edge occurs because I prewash my fabrics. During prewashing, the sizing washes out, and the fabric relaxes into a more "on-grain" state. This shift has nothing to do with the quality of the fabric. It is simply due to the way the fabric was rolled onto the bolt at the factory. There is often a good amount of waste because you loose several inches from both ends of the fabric. There is more discussion on fabric preparation in Chapter 3.

Photo 1

Now, fold the fabric one more time, fold to selvages. See photo 2. Again, you can use a motif in the print to help you fold the fabric.

If you are right-handed, place the excess fabric to your right. If you are left-handed, place the excess fabric to your left. If your fabric is more than a yard long fan-fold the excess to keep it neatly on the table.

Squaring the Fabric

The next step is to square one end of the folded fabric. “Squaring” the fabric means more than just cutting away the uneven edges. It means cutting the end of the fabric at an exact 90° angle.

Photo 3 shows a strip that was cut from an edge that was not perfectly square. Do you recognize this W-shaped strip?

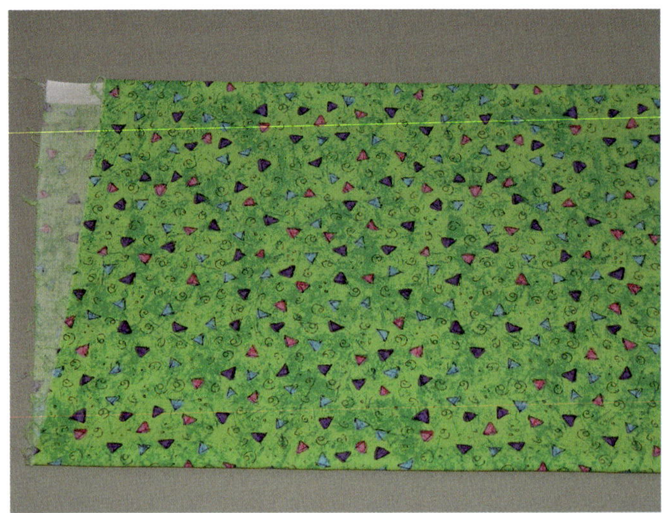

Photo 2

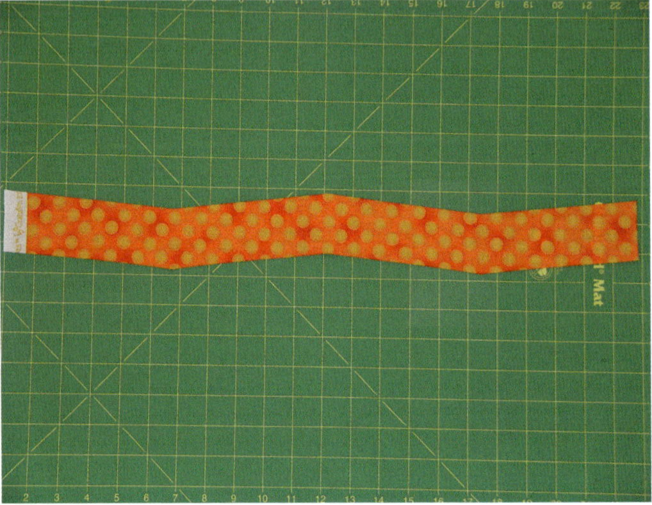

Photo 3

These wobbly strips are not the result of folding. They are the result of cutting strips from ends that are not square.

To square the end of the folded fabric, place a 15″ square on top of your fabric, aligning one of the lines of the ruler along the fold. See photo 4. In the photo I have placed the 12½″ line on the fold.

Because you are using a 15″ square, there is a long distance to follow the fold with a line on the ruler, making sure you are truly cutting at a 90° angle. A narrower ruler would not be as accurate.

At this time, walk to the opposite side of the cutting table and cut away the uneven edge. See photo 4.

Check to make sure that all four layers were squared.

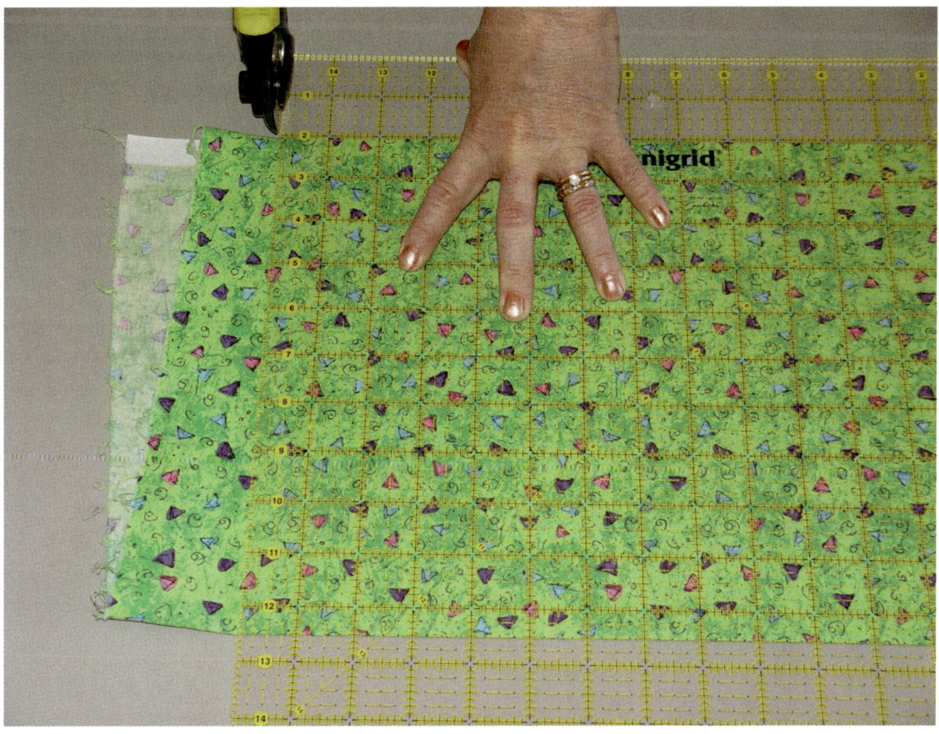

Photo 4

If you cannot walk to the opposite side of the cutting table, place the fan-folded excess fabric on the mat and rotate the mat 180° so that it will be in position to make the cut.

Now, return to the other side of the table where you began (or turn the mat back to its original position). From here you will begin to cut the strips.

Another option for those who cannot walk to the opposite side of the cutting table is to use both the 15″ square and the 6″ x 24″ rulers. Position the rulers as shown in photo 5, making sure one of the lines on the 15″ square is aligned with the fold of the fabric. Nudge the 6″ x 24″ ruler flush with the square ruler. All four layers of the raw edges should be under the 6″ x 24″ ruler. Remove the 15″ square, being careful not to disturb the 6″ x 24″ ruler. Cut along the 6″ x 24″ to square the edge of the fabric. See photo 6.

Photo 5

Photo 6

Cutting the Strips

I will use the Rail Fence pattern on page 31 for this first demonstration.

The Rail Fence cutting instructions tell you to cut fifteen 2” wide strips of fabric #1. Photo 7 shows fabric #1 after it has been folded and the end has been squared. The 15″ square ruler has been placed so that the 14″ line is aligned with the squared edge of the fabric.

Under the ruler is fourteen inches of fabric, which is enough to cut seven strips. Cut along the edge of the ruler as shown. Left-handed quilters should work in the opposite direction, starting with the squared edge on the right end of the folded fabric and sliding the ruler to the right as they cut.

NOTE: Right-handed cutters should always position the 15″ square with the 1″ lines in the upper right corner. Left-handed cutters should always position the 15″ square with the 1″ lines in the upper left corner.

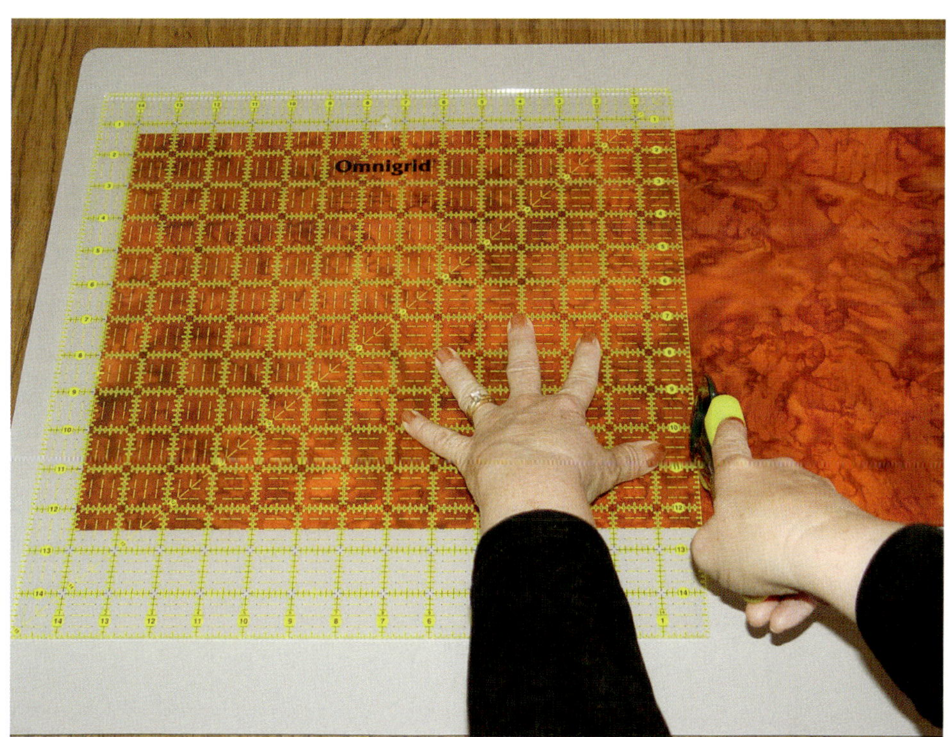

Photo 7

Now slide the ruler to the left so that the 12” line is aligned with the original straightened edge of the fabric. See photo 8. **Do not move the fabric pieces. I have separated the strips in the following photos only so that you can see where they have been cut.**

By aligning the 12″ line with the squared edge, you have revealed a 2″ strip of fabric. Cut along the edge of the ruler.

Slide the ruler another 2″ to the left and align the 10” line with the original straightened edge of the fabric. **Do not move the fabric pieces.** See photo 9. Another 2″ wide strip has been revealed. Cut along the edge of the ruler.

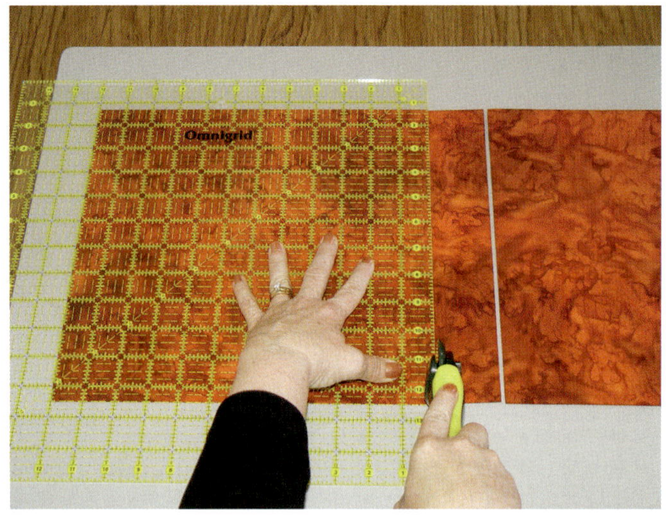

Photo 8

Photo 9

Continue sliding the ruler and cutting 2″ wide strips until all seven strips have been cut. See photo 10.

Now, pick up all seven strips and set them aside. The end of your remaining folded fabric should still be square, assuming that you did not move it while cutting the first seven strips. Place the ruler on the fabric, aligning the 14″ line with the squared edge, to begin cutting the next seven strips just as you cut the first seven.

After following the instructions from above you will have cut fourteen strips. Only one more strip is needed, so align the 2″ line with the squared edge of the folded fabric and cut it.

Your accuracy will improve as you practice this new way of moving your ruler. In the beginning you may disturb the squared edge of your fabric and need to square it again on occasion. With practice, however, you will soon be able to cut many strips without having to stop to square the edge.

Photo 10

Counting backward by two's is not difficult. It was easy for you to follow the example above where the ruler was moved 2″ at a time. The measurements that you used for cutting are what I call "target numbers". The target numbers in that example were 14″, 12″, 10″, 8″, 6″, 4″, and 2″. Once you begin to cut strips that have fractions in their measurements, like the 3½″ wide strips of background fabric needed for the Bow Ties quilt, you may want to take the time to make yourself a chart of the target numbers for that size.

Do the math one time and write the numbers down. This avoids having to calculate the measurements numerous times and avoids making cutting mistakes. Keep your lists of target numbers near your cutting table for future use. Photo 11 shows the cutting of 3½″ wide strips using the following target numbers: 14″, 10½″, 7″, and 3½″. I am using the green side of the mat because it is easier to read the ruler when cutting the white fabric. I am still measuring with the ruler and not the grid on the mat. Remember, do not move the fabric. The strips are only separated so that you can see where they have been cut.

Photo 11

Crosscutting the Strips

When cutting the pieces for a quilt, begin by cutting all of the strips required from the first fabric. After all of the strips are cut, cut them into the desired pieces. For example, to cut fabric #1 in the Three or More pattern on page 41 I first cut all of the strips (six 4½″ wide, nine 2½″ wide, and seven 1½″ wide). Then, I went back and cut the rectangles and squares that are required.

To crosscut the three 4½″ wide strips of fabric #1 into 2½″ x 4½″ rectangles I began by stacking the strips. I am comfortable cutting eight layers. I stacked the three 4½″ wide strips on top of each other. Each of the strips was folded in half, thereby creating a stack of six layers of fabric. Make sure all of the selvages are stacked on top of each other at your left, and all the folds stacked on top of each other on your right. See photo 12.

Photo 12

Use the 6″ x 24″ ruler to cut the 2½″ x 4½″ rectangles. From the opposite side of the table, trim away the selvages by squaring the ends of the strips. Walk back to the side of the table where you began and crosscut the strips into 2½″ wide sections using the following target numbers: 20″, 17½″, 15″, 12½″, 10″, 7½″, 5″, and 2½″. See photo 13.

You can crosscut the 3½″ strips of background for the Bow Ties pattern (page 45) the same way, adding 21″ and 17½″ to the beginning of the list of target numbers that were given earlier for cutting the strips with the 15″ square ruler.

Use this method of crosscutting any time you need to cut strips into squares or rectangles prior to piecing a quilt.

Photo 13

Crosscutting Pieced Panels

The appropriate method for crosscutting strip pieced panels depends on the panels themselves and how the panels will be assembled in the quilt. In the following sections, I provide several examples.

Large Blocks from Panels

The first example will use the Rail Fence pattern. For the greatest accuracy I cut wide panels that will be cut into blocks one at a time. Also, rulers are rarely large enough to provide more than one "target number" when cutting these larger blocks. I use the ruler that is best suited for the task. In this instance I used the Omnigrid® 9½″ square instead of the 15″ square because it is more convenient.

Measure the width of your panels. They should be 8″ wide. Therefore, to make square blocks, cut the panels into 8″ wide sections. Measure and cut one block at a time. See photo 14.

NOTE: The Rail Fence pattern is very forgiving. If your panel's average width was only 7½″, use that measurement to cut your blocks. This way, your pieces remain square and fit together as they are turned to make the overall design. The border blocks, however, should still be cut 6½″ wide, as directed.

Photo 14

Sections of the Same Size

All of the panels in the Framed Nine Patch pattern are cut 2″ wide. Stack a number of panels and cut them all at once. Place the first panel on the gridded side of the mat, aligning the top edge with a grid line to get it straight. See photo 15.

Place the second panel on the first one, aligning the top edge with the first seam line of the first panel. See photo 16.

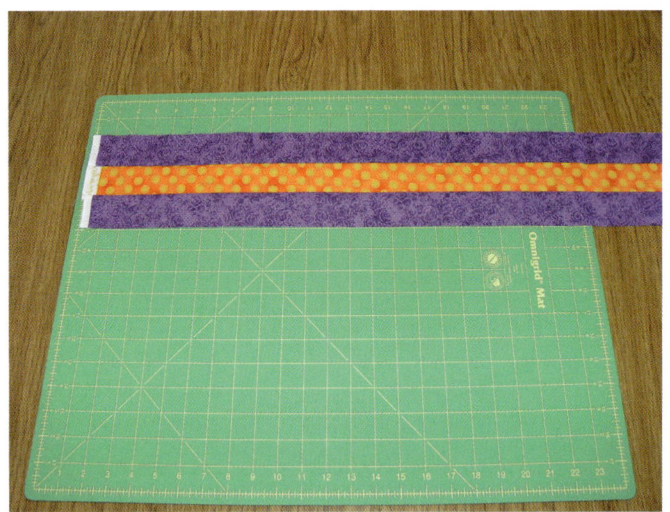

Photo 15

Photo 16

Continue layering panels, aligning the top edge of each new panel with the first seam line of the previous panel. See photo 17. Staggering the panels in this way keeps the seam allowances from stacking up in one place. Your ruler will lay flat on the panels, and the rotary cutter will roll smoothly through all of the layers.

Walk to the opposite side of the table. Position one of the lines of the 15″ square ruler along a seam line of the top panel.

Square the ends of the panels by cutting away the selvages at a 90° angle. Walk back to the other side of the cutting table and crosscut the stack of panels using 2″ increments, as you did when cutting strips from yardage. See photo 18.

Photo 17

Photo 18

Pick up the crosscut sections. Reposition and square the panels, as necessary, and continue crosscutting them into sections. Repositioning and squaring can be done less frequently if you have a large mat.

Two Fabric Four Patches

You could crosscut the panels for making the four patches in the Three or More pattern as described in the previous section. However, I choose to layer my panels differently when making four patches from two fabrics to facilitate the piecing.

Place the first panel on the gridded side of the mat, right side up, aligning the edge with a grid line to keep it straight.

Place a second panel, right sides together onto the first panel, making sure that the light fabric is on top of the dark and vice versa. See photo 19.

Feel along the seam line and make sure that it is matched along the entire length of the panels. Take time to really get the seams butted together.

Now, trim the selvages and crosscut the pair of panels into sections. The pairs are neatly matched and ready to be chain pieced to complete the four patches. There is no need to pick up two sections and match the seams individually!

Photo 19

Cutting Fat Quarters

Instead of cutting fat quarters one at a time, stack up to eight of them to make less work. Stack them in the following way: open to a single layer, right side up, selvages aligned on top of one another at the left, top edges as even as possible, and the smallest piece on top. See photo 20.

Determine whether the pattern requires you to initially cut the strips parallel to the selvages or perpendicular to the selvages. Fat quarters are not square so it is important that the strip cutting be done in the correct direction to insure that there will be enough fabric.

Photo 20

According to the directions, the fat quarters in the Bow Ties pattern on page 45 are first cut into strips parallel to the selvages. Trim away the selvages. The first strip is 6½″ wide. Start cutting the fat quarters at the bottom, using the 6½″ line on the 15″ square. See photo 21.

Cut a little more than halfway. Leave your rotary cutter anchored on the cutting mat and slide the ruler up to measure and finish the cut. See photo 22. Use this technique when you need to make long cuts that are wider than your 6″ x 24″ ruler.

Photo 21

Photo 22

Cutting Borders

Inner and outer borders are cut differently. Inner border strips are cut in the same way that strips are cut for strip piecing. Outer borders should be cut in the opposite direction, on the lengthwise grain and parallel to the selvages, so that they will not stretch and become wavy. To do so, the fabric must be folded end on end, and not selvage to selvage. The fabric will need to be folded a second time (four layers) or even a third time (eight layers) in order to make it fit on your cutting mat.

Use your 6″ x 24″ ruler to trim away the selvages from one side. Measure and cut border panels that are wider than 6″ in one of the following two ways:

Option One is to slide the ruler along as directed on page 24 for cutting the 6½″ wide strips from the fat quarters.

Option Two is to use two rulers side by side to measure the wider strip. See photo 23. The ruler on the left has the 2½″ line on the edge of the fabric. The 6″ x 24″ ruler is nudged along side of it. Cutting along the edge of the 6″ x 24″ ruler will yield a panel that is 8½″ wide.

Photo 23

Chapter Three

Fabric Preparation

Now, as I said in the introduction, this book is about cutting. On the other hand, we quilters cannot stand to cut up fabrics and not make a quilt. Therefore, I have included four patterns for quilts that use the cutting methods being discussed in this book.

Fabric Yardage Allowance

The fabric allowance for the quilt tops in these patterns is generous. One reason is because I allow for the many fabrics that are narrow, 40″ wide or less. The actual cutting instructions in the patterns assume that there is 42″ of usable width in each fabric. If your fabric is narrower than 42″ wide, you will need to cut more pieces from your excess. There will be plenty of fabric for doing so.

The fabric allowance for the quilt backing is not as generous. You may prefer to purchase your backing after you have completed your quilt top so that you know exactly how much you need for your quilt. Perhaps you will choose to add another border to enlarge your quilt. Maybe the fabric you have chosen to use on the back is a narrow one. Things like that can change the amount of backing fabric drastically.

The fabric allowance for the binding assumes that the strips are cut 3¼″ wide for a finished ½″ double binding. This is the binding that I prefer. Many quilters choose to use 2½″ wide strips for binding. Narrower bindings obviously require a little less fabric.

To Wash or Not to Wash

Today's fabrics have few problems with shrinkage and fading or running. Check any fabric that concerns you. The decision to wash fabrics or not to wash them prior to use is your decision.

I do wash and press my fabrics prior to using them. I began this habit when I first started quilting. I continue to wash them because all of my stash is washed, and I do not care to use washed and unwashed fabrics together in the same project. I have made quilts using only new, unwashed fabric; however, I prefer to use washed fabrics.

To avoid distorting your fabric as you press the yardage, move your iron in strokes which are parallel to the selvages. Pressing in this direction is with the stable warp yarns which will not stretch as you press. I often have quilters come to class with fabrics that seem to have wavy, wobbly edges along the selvages. Usually this problem is not due to the quality of the fabric. It is created by moving the iron from side to side between the selvages while applying any combination of the following: heavy pressure, steam, and starch or sizing.

Chapter Four

Basic Construction

Seam Allowances

The success of your quilts depends upon precise seam allowances. Do not believe the person who tells you that as long as you are consistent, it will be okay. Most quilts have areas of many seams as well as other areas with few seams. They must be constructed with accurate seam allowances. If you have not checked your seam allowances in the past, do so by performing the following test.

TEST: From scraps cut four 1½″ x 4½″ rectangles. Sew them together along the long edges using a scant ¼″ seam allowance. A scant ¼″ is about a needle's width narrower than a true ¼″ seam allowance. Press the seam allowances to one side. The finished piece should measure 4½″ square. See photo 24. If not, adjust your seam allowance and repeat the test.

You will notice arrows in many of the graphics of the quilt pattern instructions. These arrows show the directions that the seam allowances should be pressed.

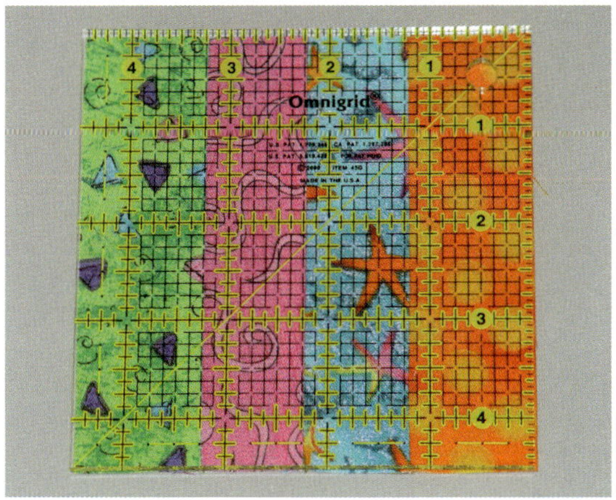

Photo 24

Strip Piecing

When strip piecing a pattern, quilters often end up with strips that curve like a rainbow. See photo 25 on the following page. This bow is caused by one or more of the following:

1. If the two strips you are sewing together are being held separately, one may be stretched more than the other. SOLUTION: Gently bring both strips together without stretching and hold the pair together.
2. If you are leaving the bottom strip on the base of your sewing machine and pulling the top one over to meet it, you are probably stretching the top strip more than the bottom strip. SOLUTION: Same as for #1.
3. The pressure on your sewing machine's presser foot may be too firm. If so, the feed dogs will feed more of the bottom strip than the top strip. SOLUTION: Consult your sewing machine manual about how to adjust the pressure on the presser foot of your sewing machine, or use an even feed presser foot if it is available.

Borders

As stated in Chapter 2 in the section on cutting borders, the outer borders of quilts should be cut with the lengthwise grain in the long direction whenever possible.

When preparing to add borders to your quilt, measuring and easing are important steps. Your quilt may not be square if you eliminate these steps. Do not just sew an extra-long strip to the side of your quilt and trim the leftovers!

Press the quilt well before measuring. As you are measuring, keep the quilt top fairly taut on a flat surface. The quilt top contains many seams, and they each have a slight amount of slack where the seam allowances are pressed to the side. The borders, however, have few or no seams and are cut along the stable lengthwise grain. Therefore, keeping the quilt taut while you measure is imperative. Measure the quilt in several places to determine its average length.

Cut two border panels to the average length of the quilt. Pin them to the sides of the quilt, matching the ends and centers, and attach them, easing as necessary. Press the seam allowances toward the borders.

Measure the width of the quilt in several places and repeat the above steps to add a top and bottom border.

If you are adding more than one border repeat the above steps for each border.

Quilting and Binding

There are books and classes devoted solely to quilting and binding. Almost every quilting magazine on the market contains basic instruction for quilting and binding in each issue. Quilting and binding are highly visible and a part of every quilt. Learn to do them well. Take advantage of classes that are available to you.

I would like to suggest you find good references. *Happy Endings*, written by Mimi Dietrich and published by That Patchwork Place, is a good book for additional information on binding. Books about quilting are plentiful. Decide what type of quilting you want to do and ask your local quilt shop for a good reference.

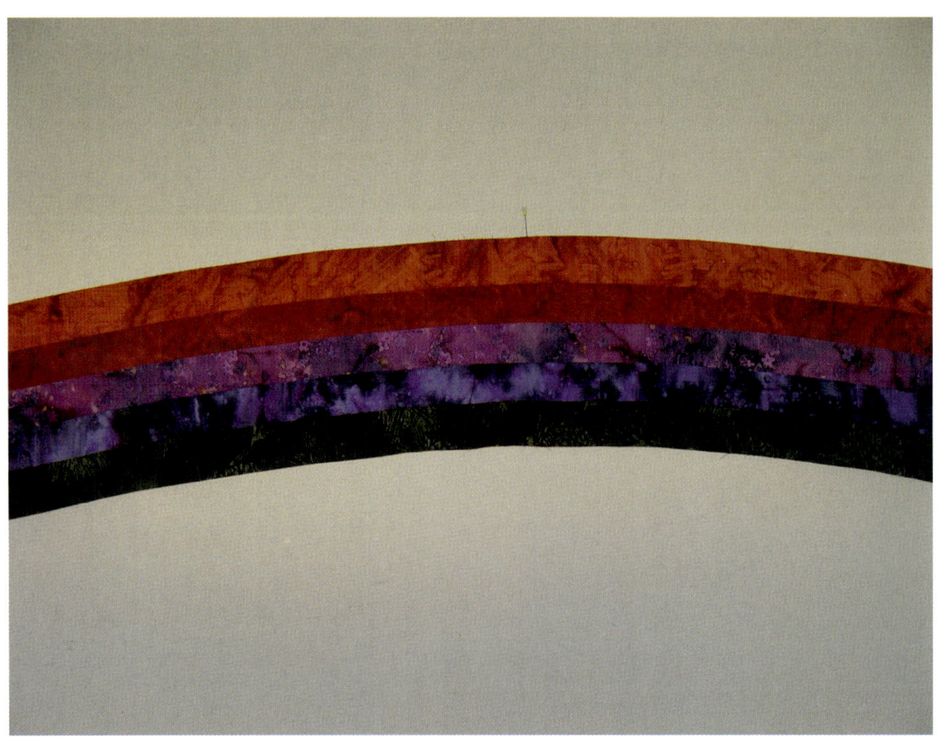

Photo 25

Chapter Five

Quilt Patterns

The directions for the following quilt patterns assume that you have read all of the basic information in the previous chapters.

These patterns were designed to employ all of the power cutting skills that were described in Chapter 2.

Learning new skills takes time and practice. Do you remember the first time you tried rotary cutting? Most of us felt awkward while trying to place the fabric, ruler, and cutter each time we made a cut. Be patient with yourself and work at learning how to Power Cut. Soon it will become second nature.

Rail Fence
pieced by Debbie Caffrey and machine quilted by Phyllis Kent

Rail Fence

The finished size of this quilt is 60″ x 75″.

The finished size of the blocks is 7½″ square.

For best results, choose and arrange your fabrics so that they begin with the lightest fabric as #1 and blend from light to dark with the darkest fabric being #5. Another suggestion is to choose colors in order as you work around the color wheel. I did a combination of the two – going around the color wheel, starting at orange, and moving from light to dark.

Fabric Requirements

Fabric #1 – Orange	1 yard
Fabric #2 – Red	1 yard
Fabric #3 – Purple	1½ yards
Fabric #4 – Dark Blue	1 yard
Fabric #5 – Dark Green	1¼ yards
Binding – More of fabric #5 or another	¾ yard
Backing	3¾ yards

Cutting

Fabric #1 – Orange

Cut fifteen strips 2″ wide.

Fabric #2 – Red

Cut fifteen strips 2″ wide.

Fabric #3 – Purple

Cut twenty-three strips 2″ wide.

Fabric #4 – Dark Blue

Cut fifteen strips 2″ wide.

Fabric #5 – Dark Green

Cut fifteen strips 2″ wide.
Cut one strip 6½″ wide.
Cut the 6½″ wide strip into four 6½″ squares for the corners of the quilt.

Strip Piecing

Arrange the strips in order, fabric #1 at the top and fabric #5 at the bottom, and sew the strips into fifteen panels like the one shown. Press the seam allowances in one direction, toward fabric #5.

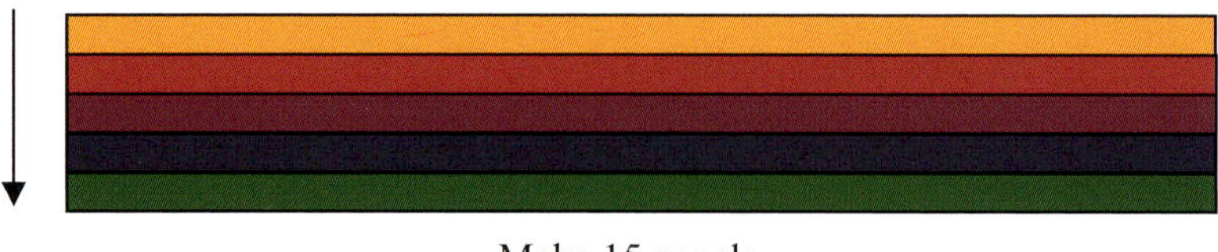

Make 15 panels

Making the Blocks

Crosscut the fifteen panels into a total of forty-eight 8″ blocks and twenty-eight 6½″ wide sections for the borders.

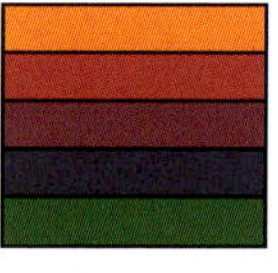

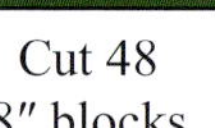

Cut 48
8″ blocks

Cut 28
6½″ border blocks

Completing the Quilt Top

Set aside the border sections.

Make four rows like the first one shown. Begin by placing a block on the left end so that the rails are horizontal and fabric #1 is at the top. The second block in the row should be positioned so that the rails are vertical and fabric #1 is at the left. Repeat this pattern with four more blocks to make the row six blocks long. Sew the blocks together and press all of the seam allowances toward the blocks with the vertical rails. These are the odd rows of the quilt.

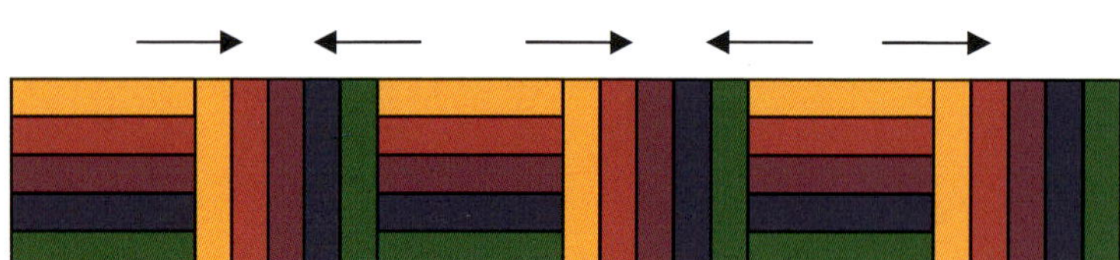

Make four rows like the second one shown. Begin by placing a block on the left end so that the rails are vertical and fabric #1 is at the left. The second block in the row should be positioned so that the rails are horizontal and fabric #1 is at the top. Repeat this pattern with four more blocks to make the row six blocks long. Sew the blocks together and press all of the seam allowances toward the blocks with the vertical rails. These are the even rows of the quilt.

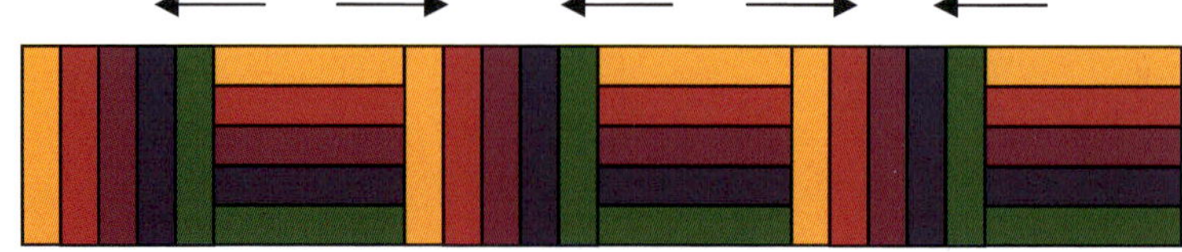

Place the odd and even rows into position to complete the pattern. Sew the rows together and press the seam allowances to one side.

Borders

Sew together eight border blocks to piece a side border. All of the blocks should be positioned with the rails horizontal and fabric #1 at the top. Refer to the photo of the quilt on page 30. Press the seam allowances to one side.

Sew two of the 2″ wide strips of fabric #3 end on end to piece an inner border. Trim the inner border to length to fit the side border. Save the pieces that you trim away for use below.

Sew the inner border and pieced border to one side of the quilt. Press both of the seam allowances toward the inner border. Repeat to attach borders to the opposite side of the quilt.

Cut four 2″x 6½″ rectangles of fabric #3 from the pieces that were saved from your inner side borders.

Piece the top and bottom borders by sewing the following units together in order: one 6½″ square of fabric #5; one 2″x 6½″rectangle of fabric #3; six border blocks, which are rotated so that fabric #1 is at the left and the rails are vertical (Refer to photo, if needed.); one 2″ x 6½″ rectangle of fabric #3; and one 6½″ square of fabric #5. Press the seam allowances to one side.

Sew two of the 2″ wide strips of fabric #3 end on end to piece an inner border. Trim its length to fit the top border. Sew the inner border and pieced border to the top of the quilt. Press both of the seam allowances toward the inner border. Repeat to attach borders to the bottom of the quilt.

Framed Nine Patch

pieced by Debbie Caffrey and machine quilted by Phyllis Kent

Framed Nine Patch

The finished size of this quilt with 7½″ wide outer borders is 64½″ x 82½″.

The finished size of the blocks is 7½″ square.

Due to the fabric placement in this quilt the nine patch units are hard to spot. Try making another variation using the chain fabric and only one additional fabric to make the nine patch center of the block. Then, "frame" the nine patches with a third fabric, using the chain fabric in the corners. Finally, use a fourth fabric for all of the sashes and the chain fabric for the cornerstones. What a difference fabric placement makes!

Fabric Requirements

Fabric #1 – Orange	⅞ yard
Fabric #2 – Turquoise	⅞ yard
Fabric #3 – Pink	⅞ yard
Fabric #4 – Green	⅞ yard
Fabric #5 – Purple	2 yards
Border	2 yards
Binding	1 yard
Backing	5 yards

Cutting

Fabric #1 – Orange

Cut one strip 8″ wide.
Cut this strip into twenty-one 2″ x 8″ rectangles.

Cut two strips 5″ wide.
Cut these strips into thirty-five 2″ x 5″ rectangles.

Cut two strips 2″ wide.

Fabric #2 – Turquoise

Cut one strip 8″ wide.
Cut this strip into twenty 2″ x 8″ rectangles.

Cut two strips 5″ wide.

Cut two strips 2″ wide.

Fabric #3 – Pink

Cut one strip 8″ wide.
Cut this strip into twenty-one 2″ x 8″ rectangles.

Cut two strips 5″ wide.
Cut these strips into thirty-five 2″ x 5″ rectangles.

Cut two strips 2″ wide.

Fabric #4 – Green

Cut one strip 8″ wide.
Cut this strip into twenty 2″ x 8″ rectangles.

Cut two strips 5″ wide.

Cut two strips 2″ wide.

Fabric #5 – Purple

Cut twenty-nine strips 2″ wide.
Use three strips to cut forty-eight 2″ squares.

Strip Piecing

Make two each of Panels A-E as shown on the next page.

Press the seam allowances of Panels A, B, and C toward fabric #5.

Press the seam allowances of Panels D and E away from fabric #5.

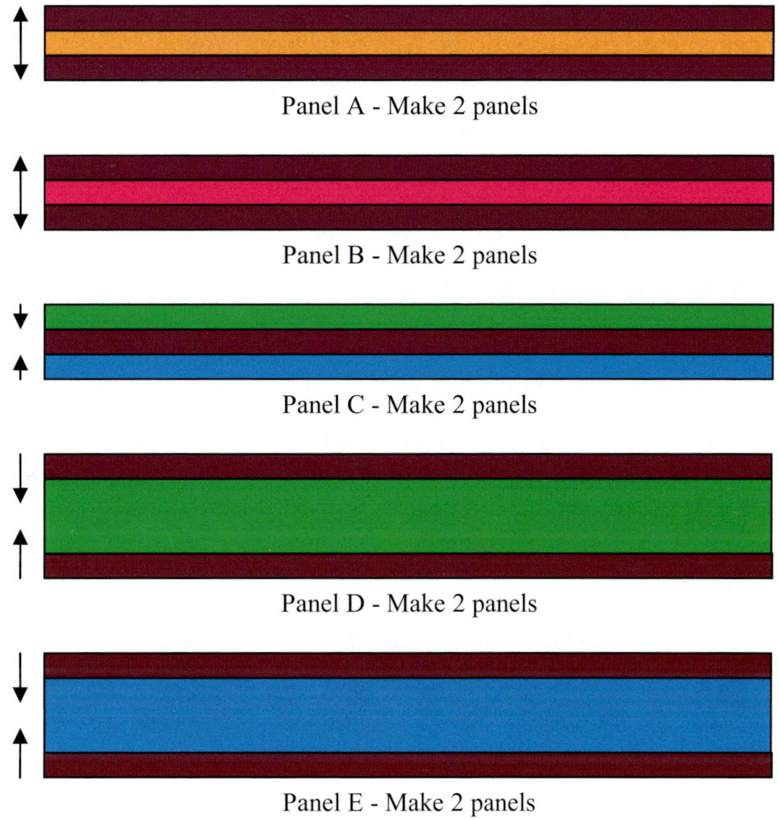

Panel A - Make 2 panels

Panel B - Make 2 panels

Panel C - Make 2 panels

Panel D - Make 2 panels

Panel E - Make 2 panels

Making the Blocks

Crosscut all of the strip pieced panels into 2″ wide sections. Cut thirty-five sections from each of the combinations – A, B, C, D, and E.

Cut 2″ wide
35 sections per combination

Sew each section from Panel A to a 2″ x 5″ rectangle of fabric #1. Press the seam allowances toward the rectangle.

Sew each section from Panel B to a 2″ x 5″ rectangle of fabric #3. Press the seam allowances toward the rectangle.

Make 35 of each unit

Sew the units from above to the sides of the sections from Panel C. Make sure you have all of the pieces positioned as shown. Press the seam allowances away from the C sections.

Make 35

Add a section from the D panels to the top of each block. Press the seam allowances toward the D sections. Add a section from the E panels to the bottom of each block. Press the seam allowances toward the E sections.

Make 35

Completing the Quilt Top

All of the block rows are constructed in the same way. Later, to make the overall pattern of the quilt, the second, fourth, and sixth block rows will be turned upside down.

Lay out the 2″ x 8″ rectangles of fabrics #1 and #3 as sashes alternating with the blocks. Pay close attention to how the blocks are positioned. Not all of them are the same. Sew together seven rows like the one shown below. Press the seam allowances toward the sashes.

Make four sashing rows as shown below, using 2″ x 8″ rectangles of fabrics #2 and #4 and 2″ squares of fabric #5 for the cornerstones. Press the seam allowances toward the sashes. Label these rows X.

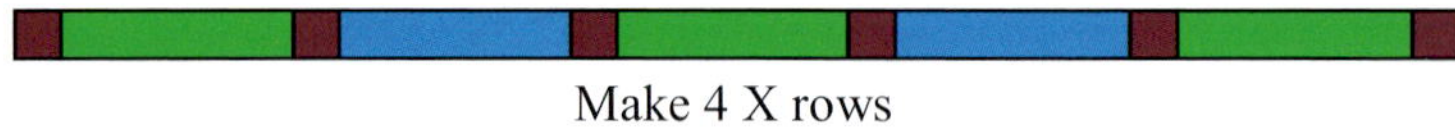
Make 4 X rows

Make four more sashing rows as shown in the next drawing, using the remaining 2″ x 8″ rectangles of fabrics #2 and #4 and 2″ squares of fabric #5. Press the seam allowances toward the sashes. Label these rows Y.

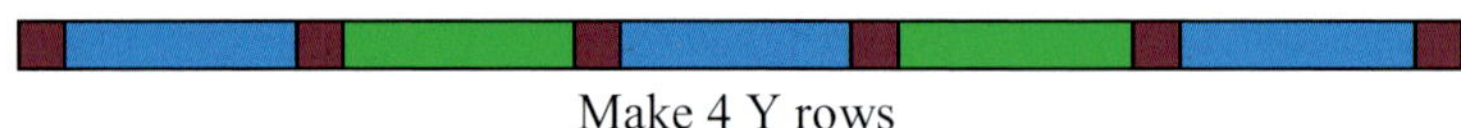
Make 4 Y rows

Lay out the rows to complete the quilt top. Start with one sashing row X at the top. Next, place a block row right side up. The next row is one of sashing row Y. This is followed by another block row, but this block row is turned upside down. Continue with this pattern to lay out the entire quilt top.

Sew the rows together. Press all of the seam allowances toward the sashing rows.

Borders

Sew the remaining eight 2″ wide strips into four pairs, end on end, to make them long enough to make the inner borders.

Remove the selvages from your border fabric and cut four lengthwise panels that are 8½″ wide. Complete the borders as directed in the general piecing instructions on page 27.

Three or More

pieced by Debbie Caffrey and machine quilted by Phyllis Kent

Three or More

The finished size of this quilt with 6″ wide borders is 60″ x 76″.

The finished size of the blocks is 8″ square.

The title of this pattern implies that you may use three fabrics, as directed, or more. For instance, it would be very attractive if you were to cut the 1½″ wide strips of Fabric #3 from one accent color and the 2½″ wide strips of Fabric #3 from a second accent fabric, creating chains of two different colors. A very scrappy quilt can be achieved by using many light fabrics for Fabric #1, many medium fabrics for Fabric #2, and many dark fabrics for Fabric #3.

Fabric Requirements

Fabric #1 – Light Blue	2 yards
Fabric #2 – Dark Blue Print	1¼ yards
Fabric #3 – Aqua	1 yard
Border – More of fabric #2 or another	2 yards
Binding – More of fabric #3 or another	¾ yard
Backing	3¾ yards

Cutting

Fabric #1 – Light Blue

Cut six strips 4½″ wide.
Use three strips to cut forty-eight 2½″ x 4½″ rectangles.

Cut nine strips 2½″ wide.
Use three strips to cut forty-eight 2½″ squares.

Cut seven strips 1½″ wide.

Fabric #2 Dark Blue Print

Cut six strips 4½″ wide.
Cut these strips into forty-eight 4½″ squares.

Cut three strips 2½″ wide.

Fabric #3 – Aqua

Cut six strips 2½″ wide.

Cut seven strips 1½″ wide.

Strip Piecing

Use three 4½″ wide strips of fabric #1 and three 2½″ wide strips of fabric #2 to make three A panels. Press the seam allowances toward fabric #1.

Use six 2½″ wide strips of fabric #1 and six 2½″ wide strips of fabric #3 to make six B panels. Press the seam allowances toward fabric #3.

Use seven 1½″ wide strips of fabric #1 and seven 1½″ wide strips of fabric #3 to make seven C panels. Press the seam allowances toward fabric #3.

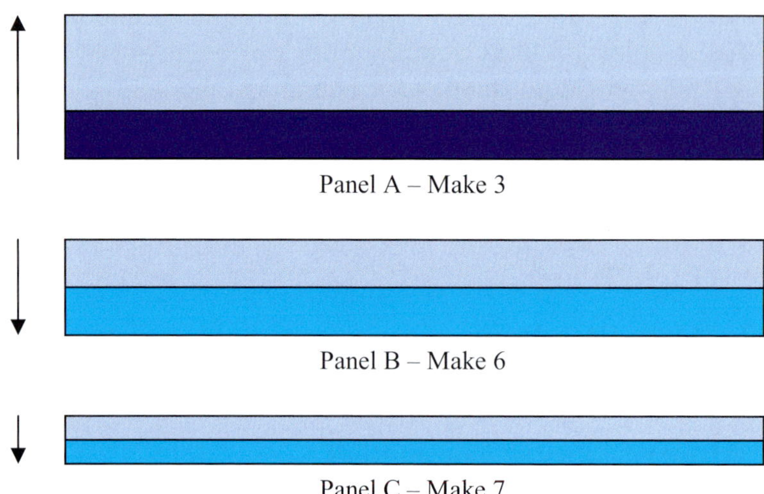

Making the Double Four Patch Blocks

Crosscut the six B panels into ninety-six 2½″ wide sections. Use these sections to piece forty-eight four patch units. Press the seam allowances to one side.

Sew each of the four patch blocks from above to a 4½″ square of fabric #2. *Make sure that the four patches are all positioned as shown.* Press the seam allowances toward the large square of fabric #2.

Sew the sections from above into pairs to complete twenty-four Double Four Patch blocks. Make sure that the fabric #3 squares form a diagonal chain through all of the blocks when they are completed. Press the seam allowances to one side.

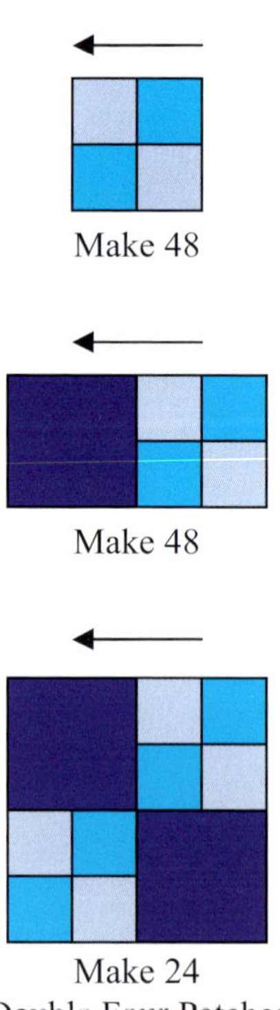

Making the Secondary Chain Blocks

Crosscut the seven C panels into 192 sections that are 1½″ wide. Use these sections to piece ninety-six small four patch units. Press the seam allowances to one side.

Sew a small four patch unit to each of the forty-eight 2½″ squares of fabric #1. *The four patches must be rotated so that the finished section looks exactly like the one shown in the second sketch.* Press the seam allowances toward the 2½″ square of fabric #1.

Sew each of the units that were just completed to a 2½″ x 4½″ rectangle of fabric #1. *Again, position the pieces exactly as shown directly at the right.* Press the seam allowances toward the rectangle of fabric #1.

Sew the units that were just completed into pairs to make twenty-four sections. Press the seam allowances to one side.

Crosscut the three A panels into forty-eight 2½″ wide sections.

Sew a small four patch unit to the end of each section that was cut from the A panels to make forty-eight units like the one shown directly at the right. *Make sure that the four patch is rotated so that the finished section looks exactly like the picture.* Press the seam allowances away from the four patch.

Complete the twenty-four Secondary Chain blocks as shown. Press the seam allowances toward the center section.

Make 24 Secondary Chain Blocks

Completing the Quilt Top

Beginning with a Secondary Chain block in the upper left corner, arrange the Double Four Patch and Secondary Chain blocks, alternately, into eight rows of six blocks. Refer to the photo on page 40.

Sew the blocks into horizontal rows. Press all of the seam allowances toward the Double Four Patch blocks. Sew the rows together. Press the seam allowances to one side.

Borders

Remove the selvages from the border fabric and cut four lengthwise panels that are 6½″ wide. Complete the borders as directed in the general piecing instructions on page 27.

Bow Ties

pieced by Debbie Caffrey and machine quilted by Phyllis Kent

Bow Ties

The finished size of this quilt is 66″ x 78″.

The finished size of the Bow Tie blocks is 6″ square.

Choosing many fabrics for a quilt can be intimidating if you have not had much experience. Fortunately, most quilt shops offer bundles of coordinated fat quarters that can help you select an array of fat quarters.

Fabric Requirements

Background #1 – White with Yellow Dots	1¼ yards
Background #2 – White on White	1 yard
Fat Quarters (18″x 20″ piece)	twenty
Binding	1 yard
Backing	4¾ yards

Cutting

Background #1 – White with Yellow Dots

Cut one strip 6½″ wide.
Cut this strip into four 6½″ squares.

Cut seven 3½″ wide strips.
Cut these strips into eighty 3½″ squares.

Background #2 – White on White

Cut seven 3½″ wide strips.
Cut these strips into eighty 3½″ squares.

Fat Quarters

Refer to the drawing at the right. Begin by removing the selvages and cutting strips parallel to the selvage edges. Cut one strip 6½″ wide, three strips 3½″wide, and one strip 2″ wide. More detailed instruction on cutting fat quarters is in Chapter Two.

Use the strips to cut the following pieces from each of the fat quarters: two 6½″ squares, twelve 3½″ squares, and eight 2″ squares.

Selvages removed from this edge.
6½″ wide strip
3½″ wide strip
3½″ wide strip
3½″ wide strip
2″ wide strip

Making Bow Tie Blocks

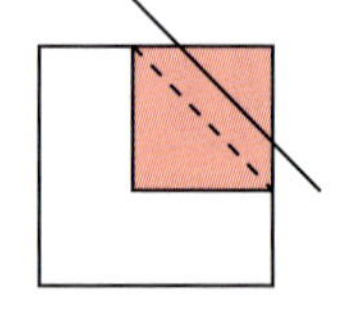

Stitch on dotted line.
Trim on solid line.

Each Bow Tie block requires the following pieces: two 3½″ squares and two 2″ squares of the same fat quarter fabric and two 3½″ squares of one of the background fabrics. Place a 2″ square of fat quarter fabric, right sides together, onto one corner of the background square. Repeat with the second of each square.

Stitch corner to corner along the diagonal of the small square. You may choose to draw the stitching lines for better accuracy. Flip the corner up to check your work. If it is correct trim away the excess, leaving ¼″ for seam allowances.

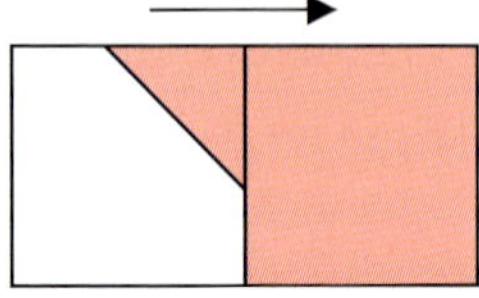

Make 2 per block

Sew each of the pieced units from above to a 3½″ square of the same fat quarter fabric. Press the seam allowances toward the 3½″ squares of fat quarter fabric.

Sew the two halves together to complete a Bow Tie block. Press the seam allowances to one side. Make eighty blocks. Forty of the blocks will use background #1, and the other forty blocks will use background #2.

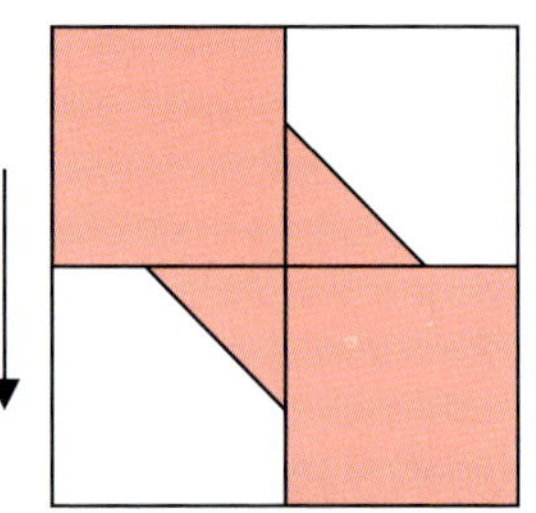

Make 80 Bow Ties

Completing the Quilt Top

Arrange the blocks into ten rows of eight blocks. Alternate the backgrounds in a checkerboard fashion. Rotate all of the blocks with background #1 a quarter turn counter-clockwise to make the overall design. Another setting option to consider is placing all of the Bow Ties so that they are going in the same direction. This arrangement will result in a strong diagonal pattern.

Sew the blocks into horizontal rows. Press the seam allowances of the odd rows to the left. Press the seam allowances of the even rows to the right.

Sew the rows together. Press the seam allowances to one side.

Borders

The inner borders are pieced from the 3½″ squares of fat quarter fabrics. Use twenty squares to piece each of the two borders for the sides of the quilt. You may choose to organize and use the squares in a specific order or use them randomly to piece the borders. Press the seam allowances to one side.

Attach the borders to the sides of the quilt. Push the seams of the borders in the opposite direction wherever necessary to make them oppose the seams of the quilt top. They can be pressed again once the border has been sewn onto the quilt.

Use eighteen 3½″ squares to piece the top inner border and eighteen more to piece the bottom inner border. Press and attach them to the quilt as you did the side borders.

The outer borders are pieced from the 6½″ squares of fat quarter fabrics. Use eleven squares for each side border. Attach the side borders, pushing the seams of the outer border wherever necessary to make them oppose the seams of the inner border. Press the seam allowances toward the outer borders.

Use nine squares and two of the 6½″ squares of background #1 to piece the top border. The background squares are placed on both ends of the border to make the corners of the quilt. Press and attach the border as before. Repeat to add the bottom border to the quilt.

About the Author

Debbie Caffrey is a self-published author of eight books and eleven patterns. In addition, she has designed and published over one hundred patterns in a frequently changing line of mystery quilts. She has taught many energy-filled workshops nationwide for guilds and shops. Some of the past venues include Houston Quilt Festival, Minnesota Quilters' Conference, Festival of Classes in Bend, Oregon, and the Road to California. In September of 2002 Debbie had the pleasure of teaching at Quiltfest in Toowoomba, Queensland, Australia, and she is looking forward to teaching in Iceland and England in 2004.

Debbie has contributed many articles to *Traditional Quiltworks* Magazine and has appeared on two episodes of HGTV's television program, *Simply Quilts*.

This fall Northcott/Monarch Fabrics will release the first line of fabrics designed by Debbie.

Debbie and her husband Dan returned to New Mexico in the fall of 2000 where they live near Santa Fe. They had lived in Anchorage, Alaska, since 1979 where they raised their children Monica, Erin, and Mark. Besides quilting, Debbie enjoys long walks and drives and experiencing new places.

In New Mexico Debbie and Dan spend many hours exploring the back roads and trails, watching the birds and animals, and studying the plants, rocks, and vistas of the Southwest.

Other Books by Debbie Caffrey

Shape Up Your Fat Quarters

Noodle Soup

Open a Can of Worms

Quilting Season

Scraps to You, Too

~~*Blocks and Quilts Everywhere!*~~ Sorry, this one is out of print.

An Alaskan Sampler

Please visit us on the web.
www.debbiescreativemoments.com